THIS CANDLEWICK BOOK BELONGS TO:

_____

_____

_____

For Jim Dowson,
a gentle man
N. D.

For Dave and Lucy
J. C.

Text copyright © 2004 by Nick Dowson
Illustrations copyright © 2004 by Jane Chapman

First U.S. paperback edition 2007

The Library of Congress has cataloged the hardcover edition as follows:
Dowson, Nick.
Tigress / Nick Dowson ; illustrated by Jane Chapman. —1st U.S. ed.
p.   cm.
Summary: A mother tigress raises two cubs and teaches them all they
need to know until they are ready to rely on themselves.
ISBN 978-0-7636-2325-8 (hardcover)
1. Tigers—Juvenile fiction. [1. Tigers—Fiction.
2. Parental behavior in animals—Fiction.
3. Animals—Infancy—Fiction.] I. Chapman, Jane, date, ill. II. Title.
PZ10.3.D735Ti 2004
[E]—dc22   2003055342

ISBN 978-0-7636-3314-1 (paperback)

2 4 6 8 10 9 7 5 3

Printed in China

This book was typeset in Poliphilus and Caslon Antique.
The illustrations were done in acrylic.

Candlewick Press
2067 Massachusetts Avenue
Cambridge, Massachusetts 02140

visit us at www.candlewick.com

CANDLEWICK PRESS
CAMBRIDGE, MASSACHUSETTS

Tigress

Nick Dowson

illustrated by Jane Chapman

Twigs with whiskers?

A tree with a tail?

Or is it a tigress,

hiding?

Tigers are rarely seen, even though they can grow as big as Shetland ponies. Tigers' bright stripes are perfect camouflage in their natural surroundings.

She can look exactly like a patch of forest, just by being there.
When she stalks slowly through leaves and shadows,
or crouches still in elephant grass,
her fiery, stripy coat seems to vanish

like **magic.**

Bigger than your fist,
her pink nose sniffs the air.

Her ears turn to listen
for the smallest noise.

Bright as torches,
her large yellow eyes
gleam all around.

Tigers don't have a great sense of smell, but their eyesight is six times better than ours, and they have amazing hearing.

8

She's searching for a new den.

Somewhere safe for young cubs.

Smooth as a river she moves.
Her plate-sized paws press the ground
but don't make a sound.
When she runs, strong muscles stretch
and ripple her body like wind on water.

She finds an untidy pile of rocks across the clearing,
full of dark cracks and crevices.
Perfect hiding for tiny cubs.

She will bring them here tonight.

Mother tigers look after their cubs alone.
So when the mothers hunt, the cubs are left unprotected.
Changing dens helps to fool predators, such as leopards
and wild dogs, that may kill the cubs.

Back at the old den, the cubs are snuggled deep in shaded sleep.

Their bright white ear spots wink like magic eyes.

With rough, wet licks from her long tongue, the tigress stirs them awake.

No one knows for sure why tigers have ear spots.
They may help small cubs to follow their mother.
Or perhaps they are flashed as
a warning to other tigers.

Grooming keeps their fur sleek and clean, but the wriggling cubs are eager to feed.
Weighing only a few pounds, baby tigers drink rich mother's milk
and fill up like fat, furry cushions.

These two are too small to walk far, so the tigress uses tooth power.
The gentle mother carries her dangling cubs, one by one,
to safety at the new den.

Tiger cubs have loose skin
on their necks, which makes
them easy to lift.

15

While the tigress hunts for food,
brother and sister stalk,
stretch, and snarl.
Teeth bared, heads together,

this could be a tiger fight.

But their knife-sharp claws are
sheathed this time and don't draw
blood. The cubs are six months
old now—when they are
older, their claws will cut
deep into the hardest wood
or the tough hide of
their prey.

Tigers can get badly hurt in fights,
so they usually avoid each other. Tigers
find their own territory, which they mark
by scratching trees and rocks and by leaving
their scent on bushes and leaves.

17

Sharp grass stems scratch three empty bellies.
For days mother and cubs have chewed old
skin and crunched cold bones.
The tigress needs a big kill, and now
the hungry year-old cubs are too big
and strong to play-hunt by the den.

A wild pig's big, bristly head bends
as his snout shoves and snuffles for grubs.
Fierce eyes burning, noses wrinkling
with his smell, the three tigers creep
closer with soft, slow steps.
They crouch, still as stone.

Young tigers start eating
meat at about eight weeks old.

19

The cubs' whiskers quiver. Their hearts thump loud as drums.
Like fire, the roaring tigress leaps and falls
in a crush of teeth and muscle.
Mouths open, her snarling
cubs rush in.

Tigers are good hunters, but even they catch their
prey only three times out of every ten attempts on average.
Tiger cubs always eat first, and if there's not much
meat, the mother may not feed at all.

Now the family will eat its fill.

The sun turns tiger fur oven-hot,
so after the big feed and a sleep,
the tigress heads for the lake.

While her cubs splash and
swim, she floats in cool,
green water to soak
away the heat.

Tigers are among the few big cats
to enjoy swimming.

Between eighteen months and three years old. tigers leave their old territory and find a new territory of their own.

Three sleek tigers prowl the midnight forest.

The tigress has taught the two cubs all her tricks.

Now, at eighteen months, they must find their own homes without her.

A pattern of gliding stripes slides into the trees,

and the mother disappears.

Brother nuzzles sister for the last time and walks away.

She watches the forest swallow his tail.

Then she turns and silently crosses the moonlit clearing.

And just like her magic mother, the young tigress

vanishes.

27

About Tigers

For years tigers were hunted and killed in large numbers, and of the eight kinds that once prowled the forests, only five survive. There are fewer than 6,000 tigers alive today, scattered across parts of China, Indonesia, India, and southeastern Russia.

Today tigers are protected, but poachers do still kill them. And people are slowly moving into the land where they live, threatening our last wild tigers with extinction.

Index

Look up the pages to find out about all these tiger things. Don't forget to look at both kinds of word—

this kind and *this kind.*

About the Author

Nick Dowson is a teacher, and this is his first book. He has always been fascinated by tigers. "Tigers are one of the creatures that sometimes roam my dreams," he says. "They are completely captivating and remain mysterious. I'd hate to see them vanish from the world."

About the Illustrator

Jane Chapman has illustrated numerous books for children, including *One Duck Stuck, One Tiny Turtle,* and *The Emperor's Egg,* named a National Science Teachers Association Outstanding Science Trade Book for Children. She thinks that tiger mothers must have a tough time in India's warm climate. "I would be so grumpy in all that heat," she says. "No wonder they spend so much time in the water!"